Building Blocks to

Becoming a Childcare

Boss

By Ineeze A Gainey

ISBN 9781730762352

Dedications

This book is dedicated to my son-shine Ammar, my dear mother Mary "Mgeez" Gainey and my father whom I miss so very much Willie Ray Gainey.

I would also like to dedicate this book to all of my Childcare Bosses in the world! I love you all.

I'm living my DREAM!

At a very young age I knew I wanted to work with children either as a teacher or a Pediatrician. Growing up in the West Park projects and "Da Bottom" of West Philly all a child could do was dream of a better life! But for me I knew I didn't want to just dream it I wanted to live it! All I would think about was is there another world outside of the one I lived in? Could there be more or even better? Living in a shelter with my mother and three siblings and other families you learn to create something from nothing. I had a crazy imagination, I was fascinated by the outdoors and by anything science related. I played a lot by myself so all I had was my thoughts and imagination, unless I was making my little sister and brother be my students as we played school in a small walk- in closet that my mother made into our toy room all of a 5 x 5 square ft. room! And if they refused then I would line up my stuffed animals, Cabbage

Patch Dolls, and Jem Dolls! I had a pointer stick that I made out of a wooden spoon and a small chalk board. For lunch I would make toasted bread with butter, cinnamon and sugar sprinkled on it with tea or Grilled cheese sandwiches that the cheese would never melt because it was from the block of government cheese and it was impossible to cut thin LOL! And on special days we would have Oodles of Noodles with cut up hotdogs! The Best!

I would talk about traveling and read to them about places I saw in the National Geographic books my mom would get in the mail. I was so amused by the different parts of the world, starring out of the 11th floor window in the West Park Projects wondering how far did the world go. As I got older my appetite for wanting more increased. When I reached high school I was placed in one of the top charters and that is where I learned about college. No one in my family had ever been to college so that language and world was foreign to me. I began to realize that this was my way out, my way to see other parts of the world and experience those captivating places I've read about!

My fire was fueled when I arrived at college. I had an expectation of myself and for my future. I understood this was the only way to get to it! I experienced things that I never imagined looking out those project windows. I met people from all walks of life and around the world. I made the most of it and I came out with a different mindset then I did going in. I had a plan long term and short term which is very important. Most of all I had a prayer! And we all know prayer without works is dead! I knew that I had so much more to still learn but I was anxious to learn whatever it took. I quickly learned that I would follow in my father's footsteps as an entrepreneur. During my senior year conducting my student teaching was when I had my ahh haa moment! I saw how restricted the teachers were in teaching their students and could not be as creative as they would like to help these children learn on whatever learning spectrum they were. To make it worst I was at a bilingual elementary school so these children's second language was English for many of them. It was very sad to see them struggle and not really able to give them the help they deserved. I then decided instead of teaching through the school district I would open up my own childcare facility, to just jump right in and plan my future and the future for my family because I was now four months pregnant with my son Ammar! So now my mindset had really changed. Now I not only had to make decisions for myself but for my child! I decided early on that I wanted to work for myself. This way I could provide the type of quality care to children without being restricted. Little did I know this decision would open the door and create the path of me becoming a Childcare Boss! Let me take you through the ABC's of setting up your empire to be your own Childcare Boss!

Acknowledgements

My place here was planned by the one and only almighty God, whom I give the highest praise of gratitude for keeping me in his presence and never giving up on me even in times I questioned him! Won't he do it!!! To my Dear Mother, I watched your struggle as well as your triumph and I honor and admire you for every stripe on your back and every step you pushed forward. I don't tell you how I feel often but I love you dearly and I know you did the best you could with the hand you were dealt! I am proud to be your daughter!

My beloved son! Oh, how we bump heads at times but you are the best decision I ever made! You make being a mother easy and I thank you. You don't say much but I see you watching and that makes me want to go harder for US! I never want you to experience the things I did and I would lay my life down to make sure you never have to! My prayer warrior friend Shani AKA Shantiqua LOL I thank God for you and always keeping me in check and on the straight and narrow! I have enormous admiration for you and your story! Thank you for always reminding me of who I am as a person, a mother and a Boss!

To all of my day 1's and my new 1's, Kwanzaa Gang Gang I love you guys to the moon and beyond you guys pull me up and never let me down! Thank you for always being supportive! My lovely Mema! Sis you already know words can't express the bond we have without words even being involved! To my Coaches thank you for the level up! To my marketing team the Nay Sayers and back stabbers I love you guys the most! To the Universe, my awareness of how important you are in my growth and being has allowed me to reach peeks that are unimaginable! NAMASTE! This spiritual ish really does work Jay!

To Pau Pau we have a love hate situation but we all know love conquers all! Thank you for investing in my dream and seeing my vision from the start. From the business pep talks and helping me come to decisions to listening to my venting and feeding me mentally and physically! Your power captivated me and your business mindset. We are both hard workers and have defeated what has been expected of us. You stimulated my mind and for that I will always be your Olivia Pope. I love you to infinity and beyond. Stay low and keep firing!

My dear father oh how I miss you so much! I know you are watching over me and I pray that I have surpassed your expectations. I know you would have been bragging and telling everyone about your Pumpkin! I remember how proud you were telling everyone your daughter was going to be a teacher when I was in college. Well dad I did a little better than that I own my own school and I make a difference for so many children and impact so many lives! There's not a day that goes by without you crossing my mind. Thank you for giving me your hustle and ambition. I know your in my corner so I have nothing to fear or lose. Let me go dad I cant type with tears in my eyes. I promise to never forget your voice. I love you daddy always your Neesa.

To my clients turned friends my little babies that listen Dymira and Jessica, I see so much of me in the two of you I can't wait to see you guys at your full potential! Dymira baby the universe is the limit I see great things for you just keep listening to Muva! Yae, sis you doing the damn thing! You're an awesome mother and no matter what God has the outcome planned. Thank you for just being you and keeping me laughing and reminding me that I'm the Shit! Wan Mitchell you always have the best advice I really admire you and I don't think you truly know! Thank you! Kimyatta thank you for your listening ear and encouraging me to get my book started! Giving me the game on being an author and adding that to my name tag! Pimp Daddy Cedes! Girl you were heaven sent God knew exactly what I was missing in my work life and connected us. You know exactly what I am thinking before I even part my lips and what I'm thinking and need done without a spoken word. I appreciate you and our bond your really are like a daughter to me. You keep me together and on track and are my biggest cheerleaders. Thank you for your strength and genuine heart!

My faithful and loyal clients, followers and supporters! Thank you for giving me that push and believing in me and inspiring me to want to keep going! Thank you for allowing me to be your Coach and Mentor, for purchasing a TEACHSHIRT, A consultation or attending a seminar or workshop! For the Dm's telling me that I inspire you guys and the many nice words that you send me daily. I am so humbled and gracious and because you all believed in me it made me want to become more to give back more. I pride myself in my work and I look at each of you as myself because I once was. You guys make me remember why I

do what I do and bring me back to my PASSION!

Table of Content

Year End Evaluation

Zeal

Three things in human life are

important: the first is to be kind: the

second is to be kind: and the third is

to be kind.

-Henry James

Attitude is Key in Business

You must have a strong mind when thinking of going into business for yourself and tough skin. Everything begins with the mind. It starts with a thought and manifests into action. We can't do anything without thinking it first no matter what it is in life. A great business person definitely thinks before they act because most business people are risk takers and know that every move has a consequence good or bad! Your attitude or mindset toward business will determine your outcome. If your stubborn and not willing to learn to grow or if you are head strong and just think people are supposed to do as you say because you are the boss (yes, they are) but it is a way of going about it and not being a you know what!

What do you expect out of your business? How do you treat your staff or clients? The key to running a successful business is treating the people that help you keep your business a float are happy and feel appreciated. Your attitude toward your staff should be caring and loving. You should never take a person for granted. Get to know your staff, find out their personal interest outside of childcare and being a teacher. This creates a personal bond and shows that you have a heart and are in tuned. Something that simple will change the atmosphere of the workplace! Instead of just having regular staff meetings try meeting outside of the space in different locations, do adventurous things (painting gallery, museum, escape room, workout etc.) or a nice restaurant!

What are your thoughts on being in business? Are they positive or negative? Remember what we think is what we bring into our lives! If all you think are negative thoughts, then why do you think you're not making any money? Why are your enrollment numbers down? How come your staff turnover is so frequent? You have to believe in what your standing for first and foremost. If you're not secure about yourself why should anyone else be! Let's start with your Passion and build your attitude around that. Put your passion to work for you and to fuel your ambition and goals for your business outcome.

Expand your mind and thought process, watch how others run their business and take good and bad notes. Be clear as to what you want to see and not see occur in your business. Get feedback from your staff and clients. Feed your mind by listening and going to seminars that are about great business strategies and can be beneficial to your business and personal self!

Think about your attitude in your business......Is it a positive or negative feeling? List your positive and negative views of your business and come up with solutions to turn the negative around!

_____

_____

_____

_____

_____

_____

What makes me have a negative attitude when dealing with my childcare business?_____

_____

_____

_____

_____

_____

_____

_____

_____

What can I possibly do to change my way of

thinking this way and create a more positive

attitude in my childcare business?

_____

_____

_____

_____

_____

_____

_____

When you come to the end of your

rope, tie a knot in it and hang on.

-Thomas Jefferson

Business Etiquette

You must hold your business to a quality of standard just as you do yourself. If you want your business to be taken seriously you must treat it as such. Even if you are running a Family Childcare business out of your home you are still running a business. Point blank period. You should have operating hours, policies and procedures that need to be abided. Stick to whatever you put in place the minute you bend you give people lead way to attempt to challenge what you have set. Then it will be even harder to try to put them back in place. Make sure that your policies are clear and cover every aspect possible. Sometimes we don't know these things until we run into them but none the less just make the adjustments as you go. This is how I learned believe it or not. I made plenty of mistakes in my business but they were learning lessons. I had no idea what I was doing but I did a lot of research. Even with research there is nothing like concrete experiences. I had a plan and I knew it wouldn't be easy but I was up for the challenge. I knew nothing about payroll, doing my own taxes, having my own insurance for my business and all of the necessary business staples I needed.

Running a business in your home which is how I started can be very difficult. You must learn to separate home and work and it can be very easy to fall into combining the two. I mean after all that's one of the reasons you began a business in your home, right? To have free will and freedom! That was one of my reasons and to be able to raise my son and spend time with him.

Even though that really didn't happen the way I planned. I will talk about that in a later chapter. You have to wrap the fact that part of your home is your business and especially with this type of business where people are entering your home on a daily bases and you are caring for other people's children you must set some standards quickly, so things are not over looked or over stepped.

You will see regardless if your childcare business is in your home or a brick and mortar your business will do much better if your setup as a business, not just on paper but in your mind and space! If you want to be taken seriously you must run a serious business. Have your business accounts setup, LLC, EIN OR TIN (Tax ID number) and Fictitious name just to say the least. Then you can set up business bank accounts and payroll and a NAV account to begin to work on your business credit! So many people want to know how to build their business credit but they haven't even set up their business correctly. It is also key to have a financial advisor, CPA and lawyer on your team and of course a COACH! Which you happen to know one that can set you up with all of these things!! Lucky you!

What are some areas in my business that I need to tighten up or even implement into my policies and procedures?

What do I need to add to my business to have it flow according to my standards?

_____

_____

_____

_____

_____

_____

_____

The great man does not think

beforehand of his words that they

may be sincere, nor of his actions

that they maybe resolute-----he

simply speaks and does what is

right.

-Mencius

Communication

We always hear the term Communication is key and it really is precedent in business. You come in contact and build relationships with many people running a childcare business. You communicate with parents, the children you are servicing, outside resources and government and municipal agencies as well as your staff every day. You must be aware of how you dictate what you expect from the people that come in and out of your facility. No matter what their role is. It is very important to be mindful of how you speak to people in general. When communicating with parents you have to put yourself on both sides of the fence and analyze things very differently. Approaching parents about their children can be a very touchy matter and it is very important to not come off as being insensitive. You want to place yourself in their shoes and be as humanly attached to their feelings and reaction. The common goal is to make the parent comfortable and not offensive toward you. Take the appropriate steps to come to an agreed upon conclusion. Offer resources and anything else that may help. When your parents feel like you have their child's best interest at hand they can trust you a lot easier. Offering daily updates about their child through some type of communication via in person through daily reports or digital reports. It is your job to make sure your parents are at ease; I mean you're only being left with their most prized possession. Parents should be able to communicate their needs to you as well. Make sure that you have periodic meetings with your parents throughout the year.

Let's not forget that staff are crucial and it all depends on how you treat them that will determine how loyal they will be and more prone to stay. It's very hard to keep staff turnover low and in this type of business keeping the same employees around is very important for the families you provide care for. Everyone wants to feel appreciated and you must show your staff that. It doesn't have to be something extravagant but comes from the heart. A simple verbal gesture of Job Well Done and pointing out something you noticed they went out of their way to do or they did extremely well!

It wouldn't hurt to do something fun with your staff to show that they mean a lot to you beyond the business. Getting to know a little more about them personally and gifting them something that pertains to their interests. Try doing fun things for meetings like ice breakers or hosting them in different atmospheres other than the job! Communication doesn't always have to be so uptight. Leave fun notes for staff or encouraging notes not only asking them to fulfill tasks but giving a pat on the back or funny joke!

How can I be more effective with my communication?

_____

_____

_____

_____

_____

_____

What are other out of box ways I can use to
communicate with staff and parents?

_____

_____

_____

_____

_____

What you do everyday matters more

than what you do every once in a

while.

-Unknown

Demanding Your Time

We as entrepreneurs always seem to bury ourselves in our work. perfecting our business and thinking of the next level. But in doing so we forget to take time to plan for ourselves to rejuvenate so that we can continue to pour into others and our business and families. It may sound silly but you may need to schedule time for yourself, I mean literally write down me time in your planner, agenda book or whatever you use to plan your day out! I didn't use to do this. I would work around the clock. I had children from morning to night in my Family Childcare Home. I didn't know how to say NO and I was on a mission. I never really took time for myself or my family for that matter. I'm still going to tell you guys about that later.

Stretching yourself too thin is really unhealthy and people tend to not care as long as you're willing. It is very imperative that you demand your time and make that very clear. As I stated before just like you plan and write down everything else make sure to write down what your business hours are and stick to them. If it's after business hours, then it just has to wait until tomorrow. This is very hard to do but you must discipline yourself and understand it's for your own good. We are always making sure everyone else around us are ok and taken care of but when it comes down to us we can't find the time. Why is that? Because as caregivers that's what's instilled in us. And I know its way easier to teach than to live it. But some things are non-negotiable.

Plan a day to yourself, an hour or two at least. Maybe get your nails and hair done. Something that small can make you feel so much better about yourself. I know if I go without getting my hair and nails done (yes sometimes it happens) especially when I'm in grind mode, I tend to not care about my appearance because I am in a different mindset. But best believe I've learned to find that time for myself! I have a special corner in my room that I go to meditate and talk with God. Yes, even that is taking time for yourself. Just taking deep breathes in through the nose and out through the mouth releasing your day and thoughts, taking time to gather your thoughts and reflect on what you accomplished today. That's another problem we have not giving ourselves enough recognition for our accomplishments.

We like to look at other people and where they are and compare or wonder why we aren't in that position. Have you ever thought about what that person may have went through to get to that point or sacrifices that were made to live that life? It's done all the time believe it or not. I always talk about how looking at someone you will never know their struggles. I grew up in the West Park Projects and before that lived in a shelter. My mother was an immigrant and was abused physically and mentally by my father before she had the knowledge and courage to leave with 4 children she stayed for a long time. But when she left she provided the best life she could for us with the hand she was given.

It's ok to sacrifice for your life, it will change you forever! Demand your time!

Make a morning and evening routine for
YOURSELF that doesn't include anyone else to
give you time to yourself and thoughts.

_____

_____

_____

_____

_____

_____

_____

_____

_____

_____

Normal is a setting on a washing machine.

-Unknown

Excelling your Mind, Business and Vision

If you have had the privilege of attending my Mastermind class you have a head start on this section! I decided to begin with the mind because I believe everything starts with the thought process. Whatever so you think will become and whatever you surround yourself with you will also become. I believe that you can adapt a lifestyle. If you want to look or speak a way you must study it to become one with it.

Your mindset all determines what your feeding it and your thought process. We have to reprogram ourselves from some of the BS we learned throughout our lives. We may not have always gotten it, and that is ok. You have to change from your old way of thinking to new thinking. You must change the way you speak about yourself and your assets around you. Using the word INVEST and not pay. Taking responsibility and not blaming others for how successful or not successful you are. The guilt blame doesn't make anything happen. You have to own up to your own accountability. Be inspired and not afraid to listen to and take direction from those that are successful and willing to share.

Invest in not only your business but yourself. Your mind needs to be fed. Your passion is fuel to your purpose and needs to be practiced as well. If you're not continuously working on your passion then your pallet will burn out. It is very necessary to stay engaged and in tune. Focus on your BIG WHY and take money out of it. We all need money so that is a no brainer. What else keeps you in your passion? Is your BIG WHY the same as your Passion? I mean really think about. Does it keep you up at night? Do you get upset when people try to down play your passion? Then you're on the right track!

You should be practicing your passion every single day. Making it better and adding on to it. Start by setting up goals and break them down into baby steps. Stop making excuses and just get to it. You're always telling yourself it's not the right time or I don't have the money or the building or the degree. But you can still start and work on building your platform.

Motivate yourself, surround yourself with likeminded people and people you want to be like. Get yourself a Coach (and I'll talk about that later), read literature and attend meaningful workshops. I love to do all of those things and I invest a great deal into myself attending workshops and putting myself in positions to rub elbows with people in high places. I never wait for anyone most business moves I do alone because if you wait for people you will miss out. Let them catch up with you, go ahead and make that move alone. I always meet great people when I attend workshops! Many of them are also alone so don't worry! If your waiting for validation from someone else then you're not ready to level up!

Don't get trapped by the people who like to play it safe. I mean don't get me wrong I usually think things through when making decisions but I also take risks. That's what being an entrepreneur consists of. So, someone that is not may not understand that. Everybody wants to be successful but many don't want to acquire the skills you need to win. But you must be committed and become focused and put effort in. Yes, you will have to work harder yes you will have to work smarter but will it pay off HELL YEAH! That achievement is priceless!

You must feel as if you deserve wealth. First think about your relationship with money. How do you feel about having and not having money? Do you know why you don't have money and complain about it or do something about it? Are you grateful to have money to pay bills, buy groceries, get your necessities etc. and show your gratitude or do you complain about having to pay bills etc. We are not taught about money or credit so most of us don't get the logistics until adulthood. Knowing that you must have a plan it's a great start to preparing your family and future!

Success can look many different ways. But no matter what Failure comes with it. I don't care who you are. I don't care how good you may think you are at your craft. But please don't discredit your failures, they are needed. They are life lessons and without failures how will you know you have grown? What does success look like to you? Is it a fancy car or a luxurious house? Maybe it's the smaller things that area really big like being able to spend time with your family and friends, going to lunch when you feel like it. Maybe success is having freedom and creating wealth, I know that's what my success looks like because everything else falls into place after that.

Show people who you are through your vision. Don't dumb down your vision because others aren't ready. I did that for so long and I was miserable. I had ideas and I wouldn't act on them and instead I would have to see someone else do it down the line. Let people catch up to you if they aren't ready. The world is always evolving and you must stay ahead of the game. Write your vision down. Sometimes it's best to see your thoughts on paper. Make a plan of how you will execute it. It may not happen all at once but prepare yourself. Begin to live and breathe your vision. How else do you expect other people to believe in it if you aren't making it believable

Your vision should be so big or at least grow each time you get close to it.

Your vision should make you uncomfortable because that means its a challenge. And thats what we want because easy things don't last.

You should always want the next level and take the steps to put you there. You can't elevate by staying in the same space. There are sacrifices and increases you have to whether as you go along in your business. No matter what never FAIL but remember its ok to FALL just don't stay down.

What are you doing to Excel your Mind, Business

and Vision?

_____

_____

_____

_____

_____

_____

_____

_____

_____

What is your BIG WHY?

Is it the same as your Purpose?

_____

_____

_____

_____

_____

_____

_____

IF PLAN "A" DOESN'T WORK,

JUST REMEMBER THE

ALPHABET HAS 25 MORE

LETTERS.

-Unknown

Financial Safety

I was always told as a business owner it's easy to start a business, the hardest part is keeping the business. So, with that said "What's the first rule in business"? I'm sure whatever it was that you were thinking is very important and prevalent to business but the answer is to never run out of money! Oh so easier said than done! Again especially if this is your first business and you're learning as you go. I've been in business for 12 years and I wish that I could say it has been smooth sailing but that would be a lie! I had no clue as to what my overhead would be or my bottom line. Your over head is the expenses you pay out each month to run your business such as payroll, supplies, utility bills, rent etc. And your bottom line is what you need to at least bring in to keep your business running.

We all know that the childcare business is a tricky business! Yes, it can be booming and your enrollment is great then all of a sudden your hit with a drought or major drop impact and you never know when it's going to happen, that's why it's so important to have a plan in place and cushion for those slow months.   Trust me I know this can be very hard to do especially if your doing it alone and you have a family and other bills outside of your business. There has been plenty of times that I had to pay bills with my credit card or payroll or even my daycare rent. I was just grateful that I had credit cards to be able to have a backup even though that may have not been the smartest choice.

Credit cards are for emergency yes but not necessarily this type of emergency! By doing this I was only setting myself back and digging a deeper hole, but I always thought well I'll just figure it out down the line. Even though I always did I should have been a bit smarter and had a better backup. I just wanted to make sure my bills were paid and my employees were paid. I didn't want to have a bad reputation with my staff of not paying them on time or all their money. I didn't cut hours when my enrollment was low which also was a big mistake and could have helped me save money. I knew people were depending on me and instead of thinking from a business stand point I thought with compassion. Sometimes compassion can kick you in your butt though! I made some changes in my payroll companies and also the way I did my payroll. Instead of biweekly I ran my payroll on the 1st and the 20th of each month and that seemed to help out tremendously. It is very important to have your staff setup with a payroll company. Shop around and see which one best fits your needs and budget as well. I did the paying under the table method but that only hurts you as the owner in the end when it's time to pay taxes. Speak to a CPA about what the best payroll option is for you and your staff.

Every time I got ahead of myself something always occurred to set me back after working so hard to get to the point I was at. Christopher "Biggie Smalls" Wallace was so right when he said more money more problems! I decided to look more into resources to help me better manage my money and business expenses. One choice was to finally stop putting things into my personal name and use my business the way I should be because I had the leverage since I was in business for some very successful years.

I began to switch out my accounts making sure that my payments that came in through my business were deposited only in to my business accounts. Making sure not to mixed the two.

This will also give you a stable and solid paper trail when you go into banks to apply for business loans and lines of credit. This gives the bank a look at how you handle your expenses and manage your money to see if they can trust you with theirs. I prefer to deal with Credit Unions personally, I feel they are more for small businesses than the larger banks.

What are some other lucrative ways that you can bring in another mean of income? Think about what you are good at, do you have a hobby or what you can invest in?

_____

_____

_____

_____

_____

_____

_____

_____

_____

You can complain

Because

Roses have thorns,

Or you can be grateful

Because thorn bushes have roses.

-Ziggy (Tom Wilson)

Gratitude Always Wins

Aaahh the secret to really winning in life is to be grateful for the big and the small! Do you really understand how far a grateful heart can take you? As Coach Stormy Wellington would say "A Grateful heart is in constant praise and worship". This is one of the rules of life that I am very big on. I do not play when it comes to gratitude because so many things and opportunities are taken for granted. We sometimes get complacent and forget where we came from. But if you're always showing gratitude you will never forget.

You should be grateful for small endeavors and free encounters as well. Especially those, just because its free and you have an abundance of it doesn't mean for you to abuse it and take advantage. Always be mindful! Remember there is always someone praying for your place and to be in position to have half the problems you have for the ones they have.

Really think about how you are showing your gratitude. What are you doing for others to let them know your grateful for their time and support? Let's talk about your childcare parents. How do you express gratitude to them? Yes, you are providing a service but a service that they could have sent their child anywhere to. Try offering a Parent Night giving parents some time to go out and enjoy a movie or some pampering time. How about offering some refreshments in the morning on their way to work or in the evening during pick up! Have incentives lined up for those parents that refer your business to new clients. I always say your parents are your best marketing strategy! Think outside of the box and be creative, it can be very inexpensive!

Now let's look deeper into your personal life and think about how you are expressing your gratitude to the universe. I start my mornings off by writing down 10 things that I am grateful for. You can start them off by saying "I am grateful for _____. Because _____. Another way maybe to say I am Blessed because_____. Also I am Thankful for_____ because _____. All of these are announcements of gratitude. As you begin to write this every day you become more aware of your surroundings and you have no time to complain. If you ever did complain a thought of gratitude comes into your mind. You will begin to see all the positive in a situation rather than pull out all the negative.

I also just randomly say thank you God for small things like my car starting every time I push that button or writing "Thank you for the money" on my bills when they come in and "Thank you paid once I pay them. This shows gratitude for what hasn't even been done yet and also for what has taken place. When you receive you should also give, it's a cycle. Even the Bible says "I will open the windows of heaven and pour you out a blessing that you will not be able to receive" When it comes to tithing so basically you have to give to receive! But you should also give without expectation or to be glorified.

Gratitude is very simple. We make things complicated. It doesn't take much to be grateful. Just look at what you have and make the best out of it and know that its someone in a worse position. You attract the things that happen to you by being or not being grateful. You can control your day or change your day by the way you think and being grateful!

"Whomsoever has gratitude for themselves will receive more and have an abundance, whomsoever does not have gratitude for themselves, what they do have will be taken away from them. I meditate and burn sage and Palo Santos and think about all that I am grateful for and all that I see coming in the future. I never ask God for anything my prayer is always of thanks. Thanking him for blessing me and keeping me and asking him to continue to do so. God knows my heart and my needs so I let him figure out when I should have them placed in my life instead of asking for it in a sense.

Make a list of 10 reasons you are grateful.

1._____

_____

2._____

_____

3._____

_____

4._____

_____

5._____

_____

6._____

_____

7._____

_____

8._____

_____

9._____

_____

10._____

_____

Some actions you can begin to do every day to show gratitude.....

1. Think about the positive in every situation

2. Write thank you for the money on incoming bills

3. Write thank you paid after paying them on the envelopes

4. Meditate/Pray every day

5. Say affirmations daily

6. Say thank you throughout the day for small tasks like your car starting or coming home to everything being in

place, having running water, food, when lying in your bed etc .

7. By blessing someone else and not telling anyone

8. By not over indulging

9. Always reminding yourself that someone else has it worse

10. Acknowledging your gratefulness

I am only one,

But still I am one.

I cannot do everything,

But still I can do something:

And because I cannot do everything,

I will not refuse to do the

something that I can do.

-Edward Everett Hale

How to keep your sanity (Core 4)

Being a Childcare Boss we all know is not easy. Tackling our daily lives, intertwining our business duties and let's not forget trying to still have a social life! We want to be around adults and not talk about lesson plans and diaper changing and what parent didn't say their child was up all night with a fever but sent them to school and covered it up by giving them medicine, like we aren't going to find out! Just as we have a daily plan and agenda organized for our children and schedule, we need to have one for ourselves in place that we follow each and every day.

 I have tried a variety of routines and I just still couldn't get everything done or touch on each day. You must find time in your day to fit family, personal, business and faith into your 24 hours. Piece of cake right? Well actually it is once you become accustomed to it!

Think about how you start your day. I want you to write down from the time you wake up to the time you go to bed what it is you do. Wake up brush teeth, take a shower, make coffee, listen to someone inspirational or however your day looks and record it add how long you spend on each activity you engage in.

Let me back up and tell you how I came to doing this method. I stumbled upon a book that someone recommended as a must read. I took their word for it and made the decision to invest (people with a growth mindset invest not buy) in the book. I could not put it down when I purchased it. I couldn't believe that this book had the answer to all my problems!

And from that day on I put those practices into place and my life has not been the same since! There are four areas that pretty much make up our life. These areas we cannot live without and how much energy we put into each determines our days outcome.

Here are the categories and it's up to you to put them in to order of importance to you. Body, relationships, business and your mind. I loved the concept that this book gave when speaking about your mind because I do believe everything is done in the mind. It begins with a thought. Me doing this book and all the events I have had began with a thought put into action. When you figure out your WHY your HOW becomes so much easier. You must train your mind to believe in what you want for yourselves and be willing to invest and sacrifice when it comes.

Once you have mastered wrapping your head around that everything in your daily routine stems from your mind, it is easy to grasp the other three concepts. You control what goes into your mind and what you do with it is the real test. If we want to waste our minds by doing nonsense things that's exactly the type of mindset we will create. By elaborating on what we study and explore that's what helps our mindset grow. Just as a garden needs to be tended to in order to grow and produce whatever was planted in that garden, those actions have to occur. You can't base it off of what the plant or tree is suppose to produce. You can only go by what becomes of it. A garden can't grow in desert climate. It's extremely hot, no shade to protect it no water to pour into it! So what do you think will become of this garden? It will eventually wilt away and have no purpose. But a garden that is nurtured, fed and watered will grow and sometimes grow so wild and beyond its space in a pot it has to be removed so it has room to expand and become of its full potential! I felt this way with the people that I was surrounded by. I didn't feel nurtured, I didn't have many people around me that had the same mindset that I had.I wasn't being fed on the level that I needed to flourish. I began to travel to seminars and workshops and that's when I knew what I had was bigger than my placement that I was in at that moment.

I began to make other connections but as I made those connections of course old connections began to drift and eventually fall off. In order to elevate you must let go of dead weight that can become no use to where you are going. My mindset began to change and I began to think, talk and my wants became different. Now that I was clear with my mind and I was feeding it appropriately and daily with positive content my mind was more at ease and decisions became easier.

Now I could work on my relationships with the people around me. Noticing which contacts were genuine, which contacts I should leave alone and which ones I have outgrown.

Write your daily routine from the time you wake up to the time you go to bed and include each aspect of the Core 4 into each day.

_____

_____

_____

_____

_____

_____

_____

Entrepreneurship is less about

Your product and all about your

Discipline

-Unknown

Juggling Family and Business

Believe it or not this is the hardest part for me in being an entrepreneur. I have always struggled with balancing the two. I still do struggle and I honestly don't know if I ever will have a handle on it, but I have gotten better. In order to do so I had to cut back though. So let me explain my situation to you guys. I started my Family Childcare business when my son was about two years old. He was in daycare prior to me starting my business with a dear friend/sister to me now that I hold close to my heart. She was the only person that was willing to give me some guidance when I was starting out in the childcare game. She knows who she is and I will forever love her for that! So while my child was in childcare I worked for an Agency in a school setting with children on the Autism Spectrum. I loved my job but I knew it wasn't what I really wanted to do.

So I began to research and do my homework on opening a Family Childcare Facility. When the time came that I felt that I was ready I decided to make my transformation during the summer of 2007 while I was on summer work with my client, because my hours were more flexible than during the school year. I was able to bring my client home with me and still work on opening my business. I was very scared and nervous just as anyone would be starting something new. However I was very confident in myself! By the end of the summer I basically had no choice but to leave my job because my childcare facility was basically full. I had 4 children and It was only myself at the time so there was no other option. I left my job and began to walk into my destiny!

I had no clue as to how to really run a business. I just knew what my passion was and my BIG WHY and I had determination. I soon withdrew my son from his daycare since now I was all in so he stayed home with me. Even though I thought plenty of times to send him back! Because he was out of control, he didn't want to share with the other children, he wanted to do what he wanted. Now remember this is his house too so he couldn't wrap his mind around why these kids were in his space and playing with what he thought was his toys and sharing his mother! I decided not to send him back and keep him with me because he would have to eventually learn.

I still get emotional when I think about this part of my entrepreneur life. Many people don't understand and will never know the sacrifices you make being an entrepreneur. I knew that you do not get what you wish for, you get what you work for. And that's exactly what I did. I hustled from morning to night. I worked on and in my business every day on top of being a mother and fiancé too. I wasn't a single mother at the time I was still in a relationship with my sons' father.

We were engaged and living together. He had a great job working as a Juvenile Probation Officer and made good money and so was I.

My business grew very quickly and soon I had children all throughout the day into the evenings. My day was spent tending to other people's children and halfway to mine. Often when he would be distracting or acting out I would simply send him off to his room. Not thinking about how that must have made him feel, to be shut out when all he wanted to do was be a kid. But I was in work mode not thinking or realizing. This is still very hard for me to think about; I've cried the whole time of writing this chapter. I feel guilty and mad and ashamed. I was trying to do good but I really was neglecting my son in a sense. I didn't think anything about it because he had the want for nothing. I bought him everything, he had the best of the best. We went everywhere, he had the best birthday parties, traveling and all. I mean no was never an option.

I loved my son and I thought this was the way to show him because I never got to experience many of these things as a child. I wanted to make sure that he never endured the things I did or ever wondered what certain things were like. I compensated my time with gifts. I did the same thing with my relationship. My attention was always with the kids or my girlfriends. You know being in the house all day whenever I could I would go hang with my then friends. I still did my household duties. Dinner was cooked and his plate in the microwave and the house stayed clean. I thought that was good enough! My son began playing sports very young at the age of 3 years old, I wasn't able to make his practices and games because I was usually working.

His dad was a coach so he would accompany him to practice and his games. So, I still didn't think anything of it and not only realizing I wasn't being supportive of my fiancé either. I was just so buried in my business.

It wasn't until my son began preschool and I had a conference with his teacher because she was bumping heads with him for some reason and I never had a problem with his last teacher about his behavior. We talked about the issues she was having with him and she proceeded to ask if he was doing any of these things at home and I told her only some of the behaviors she had mentioned but nothing disrespectful. She then asked me what my occupation was and I told her I was a childcare provider. She then asked me when he acts up at home what do I typically do and I responded usually send him to his room. She then began to point out to me how that was a problem and how I didn't seem to get why. At that moment was when I finally realized that I was shutting my son out and didn't even know that I was creating resentment in him at such a young age and this is why he was acting out in school because he wanted attention.

Now here is this child that while I was pregnant I did the most. I made a belly cast, I watched all the episodes of A Baby Story and Birth-Day on the Discovery channel! I read the "What to do when you're expecting" all-time favorite book of first time moms! I wanted to have every gadget and do every class and have a water birth and all the other cliché mommy to be things.

I couldn't wait until he got here to see who he looked like and to finally tell him I love you to his face. And to think that this is what I was doing to my child devastated me. From that day on I decided to make a plan. I decided to hire staff to help me out in the daycare and to free up some of my time to be able to spend with my son. I forgot one of the reasons I created this lifestyle was to have freedom and I wasn't taking advantage of that.

Sometimes I have to catch myself because I fall into this state of mind whenever I'm super focused on an idea. I quickly check myself and remember to follow the Core 4! I had the heart to finally ask my son how he felt about me running a childcare business and it broke me down. I wasn't really ready or expecting my son to give me the response he gave me. I asked "Son do you resent me for running a childcare business"? He is now 13 years old so he understands the question very well. He replied by saying "No, but it is in the way sometimes when I want to do things with you". Like what? I said with a heavy feeling in my chest. "Sometimes I couldn't come downstairs, and sometimes I also feel like you care more about the kids". My heart sank. No parent ever wants their child to feel that something or someone is more important to them then they are. I was devastated, I felt a huge knot forming in my throat and major guilt. He continued by saying "Sometimes you forget to pick me up or your running late because you're so busy with the kids". The tears began to roll down my face and my mind went back to that place when I was in hustle mode. I thought to myself I can't believe he remembers and here I am doing it again.

Even my relationship with his father was diminishing. I wasn't giving him much attention, I was burying myself in my work. I tend to isolate myself when I am in deep thought. I learned a lot through this time and I have come to the realization that whoever I end up with has to be a strong-minded business man LOL! I feel that they are the only ones that understand the life of a serial entrepreneur! I made a promise to myself and my son that I would always make time for him no matter what. Following the Core 4 has helped me tremendously with that!

What do you find is most challenging in your childcare business when it comes to balancing family and being an entrepreneur? What do you have to lose? How can it hurt your family or business?

_____

_____

_____

_____

_____

_____

_____

_____

_____

Create a plan so that you are giving your family the time and attention they need without missing a beat within your business. Do you think that's even possible?

_____

_____

_____

_____

_____

_____

_____

_____

_____

_____

_____

FEAR CAN KEEP US UP ALL NIGHT

LONG, BUT FAITH MAKES ONE

FINRE PILLOW.

-UNKNOWN

Keeping the Faith

There has been so many times I wanted to give up. I felt lonely and frustrated. I had no one to turn to to share my frustration. And the friends I had wouldn't understand what I was talking about. Also fighting with the fact that you really don't want others to know what your going through and label you as week because you are far from that but just wanted a shoulder to cry on.

You quickly find out who your God is and what he is capable of. When your at your lowest darkest moments and even at your highest level of your seasons moment you should praise him the same. God sees all your troubles so why wouldn't you speak to him. Why wouldn't you confide in him? Has he ever put you in situations that he didn't pull you out of or even teach you a lesson?

We must have a routine with that also includes God our creator. It's good to have friends and family you are able to go to but no one will take care of you like God will. He won't judge you, he won't tell you I told you so and remind you of all the mistakes you made. He listens and if your quiet and still enough he will talk back. If you are a religious or spiritual person you should include it in your business as well! God is all over he is in everything we do and create.

It is very important to pray over your business. Just like you want and pray for protection over yourself and your family you should be doing the same within your business. It's a tough world out here and we need all the guidance and support we can get. I owe God for all the success I have been exposed to. For giving me exactly what I prayed for and more.

It is a must that you are very specific when praying to God yes he knows your heart but it means so much more when you express it to him and make it clear. I don't think I am the greatest prayer but I get my point across even if sometimes I have to write it out first! Go to him with an open grateful heart and it always doesn't have to involve you wanting something just be appreciative!

I don't really consider myself to be a religious person. Yes, I go to church sometimes and I watch online when I can't make it. But I feel like I am a more spiritual person as most of you that follow me know. I grew up in a spiritual and religious home so I was exposed to both. My mother lit candles but as a child I didn't really know the significants of it. I knew they lit candles in catholic church which was my mothers religion she brought us up under.

We attended catholic school all of our elementary years. That's one thing for certain my mother was determined we had a good education even though we lived in the projects we went to St. Ignatius of Loyola Catholic school. I had some good years there as well as some trying years, Trying to find out who I was as a person. Trying to be with the it crowd, well what I thought was the it crew of girls. Even in the group of friends I had I was the underdog. I went through that in my high school days as well just trying to find my way. I had older sisters but not close enough to confide in so I had to figure things out on my own. Well I don't think I did too bad!

We went to church regularly on Sundays and I hated it I didn't feel a connection, I barely paid attention. Then I was introduced to the baptist church when I was in college by my son's paternal grandmother. I loved every moment of it the singing the preaching it was just something about being there that lifted my spirit. I continued to go back sometimes I would slip and find myself not going then as soon as something tragic happens in my life I'd go crawling back and every time God would be there with open arms! And I felt it. I began to really pay attention and really look at my life and really understand how God has covered me.

But I also had a connection with the Universe, my father was a reader. Yes, a psychic! That's how he met my mother. So I would see him light candles as well at his house and would always see these little jars of oil but I thought they were cologne or perfume! He would rub them on my hands sometimes, I didn't know what it was for I just thought oh these smell good lol I'll never forget when my father told me I was pregnant and I was only a few weeks maybe a month! That blew me away!

My mother never told me what my father was until he passed away and that made me ask questions and begin to research that side of who I was. I never felt a peace like that before. Learning and talking about the different deities and gods. Learning about what different colors and candles and number symbolism, it opened up a new world to me. I kept this part of me to myself for a very long time because I knew many would not understand. And I you don't believe the Universe has anything to do with your steps you wouldn't understand!

I owe so much to my Lord and Savior and the Universe. I believe what you put out you receive. What you ask of the world it will give to you as long as your grateful and have an open heart! I burn candles regularly for all different reasons! For my protection, my faith, for love and to cover my business. I have even burned candles to bring forth my manifestations in my life. From getting approved for loans to finding both of my childcare facilities and more!

I believe in manifestation. If so you believe it you shall obtain it. If you begin to really pray on something and put works behind it it will begin to happen. I remember manifesting my car, writing down exactly what I wanted from the color to the interior and the make, model and year. I began to write affirmations as if it was already done. When I tell you when your more conscious and aware you begin to notice things. I would see about 30 to 50 of this particular car each day it was so crazy because I never noticed before, now it seemed like everybody had this particular car! Then I finally got it!

When you pray to God no matter your religion and you show a grateful heart he will bless you hands down! Its moment when I want to throw in the towel, pull my hair out and throw the whole daycare in the trash!   I really would be frustrated and drained and -stressed out, but no one would ever know. I hold it all together by the strength of God. At timers I really truly don't know how. Trying to keep up with my mortgage and paying rent and bills at both locations, tuition for my son, payroll and everything that life throws at you.

You really just want to crawl in a hole and wish it all away. But there is always this little bug on your shoulder that keeps pushing you telling you it's not possible for you to give up. That can never happen, you know how many people are relying on you and looking at you. You can't disappoint them. You can't let the haters have their way. I sometimes don't know how I am going to get from one side to the next. I know my dream is bigger than what the world is ready for. I understand the struggles I have to go through to get there but damn sometimes the struggle is really real and you don't want to go through them.

But then if you didn't how could you give your testimony? How could that next childcare boss follow in your footsteps and know what steps not to take if you didn't take them for her? What will your children do if they saw you? How weak will you sound if you told someone? Then you strap up your boots and you listen to what God told you how he will never fore sake you and how if you listened to him just listen to him everything will be okay! Psalm 37:4-5 reads "Delight yourself in the Lord , and he will give you the desires of your heart.

Commit your way to the lord; trust in him, and he will act."

Just listen to him and he will make sure your okay! Don't listen to yourself. Don't listen to your peers nor your family but listen to him and commit to his ways and he will act!

What ways do you keep your faith?

_____

_____

_____

_____

_____

_____

_____

_____

You were born an original, don't

become a copy.

-Dustin

Looking Outside the Box

I'm sure no matter where you are in the world childcare is booming and a lucrative business to have. Many families need childcare, babies are never going out of style and it will be a business that will continue to grow. I want you to sit back and evaluate your business and see if you are meeting your expectations or do you have room for improvement. Well, let me tell you that even if you feel that you are meeting your expectations there is always room for improvement and growth. But what makes you stand out? What are you doing that's a little more different then the childcare facility down the block? What are you doing to draw clients to your facility? How are you reaching your market? What does a tour look like for a family that is interested in your business?

Ok, so let's think outside the box! Marketing is an important key for any business. Make sure it's fun not just your regular flyers or newspaper ads but do something that makes people look! Cover all areas on social media! Create a Facebook and Instagram account. Some clients may only use one platform and you don't want to leave them out or not reach potential clients. Do a commercial ad that you can show periodically on your social media platform. Have parents do testimonials or testimonial videos or written statements about your childcare facility. Word of mouth is the best marketing tool. When a parent talks about you that will go a long way. You gain accredability through reviews from your clients. You can do cards and have a drop box for them to place them in. Ask them if its ok to use it in your marketing materials and website. Make it real it doesn't have to be staged or pre-rehearsed. Just a simple question as to "Tell me why you chose our childcare service?"

You can do childcare brochures I like to use these to give to prospective parents instead of giving away my enrollment folders if the client isn't exactly sure if they are enrolling or basically hasn't paid the registration fee. If they pay the fee it shows commitment and then at that moment I will provide the client with an enrollment packet. List all the items that you provide outside of quality care because everyone says they offer quality care. List your differences and unique benefits that you offer such as your space your transportation your meals, security system weekend care, second shift etc. You can also put a few parent testimonials in your brochures and accreditations or awards your facility may have received. A call to action is a must such as coming in for a tour or take advantage of our free day of care or 2 hours of care. Include special offers like discounts for siblings too.

During Halloween create goody bags to pass out with your business card inside. Attach a sticker version of your business card to the inside of a book and give them away at open houses or clinics and libraries and anywhere that has a waiting room and caters to children!

I never thought about running ads and campaigns on Facebook and Instagram but this investment is worth it. Take a few dollars to invest in your advertising or boost a post you made that may be doing good.

Think of some strategies that you aren't using in your business that you could implement to help increase your exposure. Keep track of what's working and what's not.

_____

_____

_____

_____

_____

_____

_____

_____

_____

The Universe is what You

illustrate it to be .

-Rory

Manifesting

As I explained in an earlier chapter, your mind begins the process of bringing your thoughts and dreams alive. There are steps that we need to take in our lives in order to get what we want and receive the outcomes we are looking forward to. This is called manifesting. Manifesting is simply attracting what you want by controlling your thoughts and mind. It is the act of being clear of what's on your mind and what you want to see happen. You can manifest anything into your life. I practice manifestation all the time. And if you believe it really works but you have to be consistent and open minded. Manifesting consists of a number of actions being taken. I usually start by meditating sitting in a quiet space with just my thoughts. I write out what it is that I would like to manifest so that I am very clear with my thoughts. I owe plenty of what I have and what has occurred in my life to manifestation.

These are some of the actions I take. You can play soft music or frequency music in the background if you like, Close your eyes and take deep breathes in through your nose and out through your mouth. With each breathe imagine yourself getting lighter. Release all negative thoughts and inhale positivity, awareness and connection. These breathes help you become one with yourself and your thoughts. Begin to envision what it is your manifesting be exact with It down to the color or amount and be descriptive. Imagine yourself already in It, already enjoying It! Each day meditate and write in your journal about what your manifesting but use your words as if you already have it in your possession. If you pray, pray about it ask God to open your heart and mind to it. Say affirmations daily! I do this everyday for 28 days and just about always if I'm really focused I get what I manifested!

Affirmations are powerful because words are powerful! When you speak such a thing you are putting it out into the universe it's no longer just within you so there for It can become of substance. If you repeat something often enough you begin to believe It be It a lie or something you want. And when you begin to believe It your actions begin to shift to align with your train of thoughts. You want to position yourself to be in places that will help you grow into your new space. You begin to think differently. The people you surround yourself with will change. You won't want to associate with people that you don't have a common ground with.

You get bored and uninterested in spending time with anyone that doesn't have the same thought process that you have on life. People that you may have known all your life become a non factor. You want to burry yourself in literature that feeds your mind and attending workshops to surround yourself with people that want the same as you. This is how you know your affirmations are working. You must psych the mind out first. Rid your thoughts and vocabulary of negative language. Remember to seek gratitude in every situation no matter what.

Only you have control over your life. Your decisions produce your outcomes, no one can make you do anything! Yes sometimes It hard and we react off of impulse. But we ultimately decide.

There is a connection between hand and brain and interpreting what you want mixed with your energy is a powerful thing. So again you can do this by manifesting your business, business location, type of clients and staff you want etc. Write it out and say it every day, don't just write it and forget about it. You must be very clear on what it is you want, your ideal details and vision. Watch how things begin to unfold!

Ask yourself what do you want to manifest Into your life?

_____

_____

_____

_____

_____

_____

_____

Write down what's holding you back from receiving this in your life.

_____

_____

Write down why you are deserving of this in your life.

_____

List 2 books that will change your mindset to become more powerful

1._____

_____

2._____

_____

YouTube frequency music and meditate for about 5-10 minutes envision yourself in the space you want to be and doing and living. Write how you felt after meditating.

_____

_____

_____

_____

_____

Here are some Affirmations that I say every day that I received from my Coach

Coach Stormy Wellington

I AM A CHAMPION

EVERYTHING I TOUCH TURNS TO GOLD

ITS MY TURN

ITS MY SEASON

I AM HUMBLE

I AM HAPPY

I AM WEALTHY

I AM STRONG I WILL HEAR THE VOICE OF THE HOLY SPIRIT

WITHIN

I WILL LEAD AND NOT FOLLOW

I WILL CREATE AND NOT DESTROY

I DEFY THE ODDS

When you're up in Life, your
friends get to know who you are.
When you're down in life you get to
know who your friends are.

-UNKNOWN

Naysayers are the best reason to Never Give Up

When we are excited about our dreams and aspirations in life and we share them with the people we love we expect them to be happy for us. So sad that the people that are the closest to you are the ones that want to see the worse happen to you. Your so called childhood friends, family and loved ones. Yes even the person your dating or even married to will try to talk you out of your dreams. Don't allow anyone to cloud your thoughts, remove the word no or impossible. Majority of the time those people have never even tried what your trying to do or even see your vision. Don't apologize for your ideas and lose yourself or even give any energy to those negative people. They will tell you all types of stuff. Everyone is doing that. You don't even have the money to start a business. That's too hard, you won/t have a life. Well do you think that anyone that started as business didn't think those things too but decided to go for it anyway.

I stepped out on faith but I did the first step.......showing up! I was willing and present maybe not totally prepared however that is ok. You learn along the way. Just step out and do it then figure it out as you get to it. Whatever motivates you use that to push you. Wether its being broke, material or just wanting to accomplish what you set out to do. Your friends will be upset because they feel that your neglecting them and your changing. I have never heard that change was a bad thing. When God is shifting you he doesn't just shift one aspect of your life it begins to trickle down through your everyday interactions, the way you speak, the way you look at different moments in your life. You begin to look at other people differently too, they become weird and foreign to you.

Everyone has an opinion and thats fine. However, you don't have to listen to everyone's opinion either. Never allow people that gave up on their dreams talk you out of yours. You make your decisions and can handle you own decisions. Let them know you will ask for their opinion when you need it. Opinions are the cheapest commodity on earth. Don't do whats best for others, they will discourage you because they don't want you to become more. Once you become more you become disconnected with them. Then the hate begins. Keep your high standards.

I have lost people along my journey but I embrace my critics because they helped me with my success. Like WALLO says "Haters is your marketing team so let them hate." Thats why its so important to cover yourself and protect your energy. They only see you as a threat so they attack you and try to tear you down for their personal selfish reasons.

Are you a pushover? I didn't think so! So why the hell would you let them discourage you to be more like them. Those "realist" that always have a matter of fact mentality.

I learned to build a life that said I told you so without having to speak. I let my actions do the talking that's another reason why I am so successful. I am not only successful monetarily but mentally and that part took some time to reach. I use to let what people said get under my skin, it definitely would bother me. I remember telling a guy I was dating at the time when I made my first six figures in my home daycare how excited I was. In return instead of celebrating my accomplishment he responded saying but you don't have six figures in your bank account. He may have been right however to me that was still a major accomplishment because that meant that I was that much closer to being there so it didn't matter. In turn it pushed me and made me want to make that one of my goals.

How do you make it and overcome the odds? Well you can stay there and get kicked down or you can dream, get your butt kicked then start over! You have some people to shut up so get out there and get what you want. Make it a must, it has to happen.

What are you going to do to block out those

naysayers in life?

_____

_____

_____

_____

_____

_____

_____

_____

What are some responses you can give to family or friends that are telling you to give up on your dreams?

_____

_____

_____

_____

_____

_____

Entrepreneurship is less about your product and all about your discipline.

-Common Ground Management

Organizing Your Childcare Business

Don't you just love all the paperwork that comes with running a childcare business! Of course not! That is why it is very important to have task management and file strategies in place for your staff and also the children you take care of. You should know how to track your enrollment and what is your bottom line. This is where your business hat will come into play. Make it plain and simple where as anyone that came on board your team would understand fairly easy.

You must begin with your staff. Everyone on your staff should be on the same page and also should have input into the strategies and policies and procedures set forth. Have meetings with your staff at least monthly however if need be you can do weekly brief meetings with your head teacher for the following week. When you include your staff into the policy makings they tend to stick to it and enforce them even more. Have them help you come up with topics because sometimes we are only thinking with our director hat and not as an employee looking in.

Do you have a system in place for enrolling children? Do you have a form that your staff feel out when a potential client calls about childcare. This list should include space to write the potential clients full name, address, contact number, the child's name and age, email address and if the client is private pay or subsidy. You will use this list to create your ongoing list to do follow ups for the future. Along with this list you should have a telephone script in place for your staff when taking phone calls from potential clients. This way you know exactly what is being said to these clients and nothing is left out and a tour is setup and sealed. You never want to give information out about your facility until you have received the callers information. This way they can not hang up right after you answer their question and now you have their contact to do a follow up with them. The script should be to the point however very professional and pull the client in to come for a tour right away. Always have some kind of call to action or special to get their attention.

Before I began to use this strategy, I would be scrambling and panicking when my enrollment dropped. Then I would try to put a open house together quickly and desperately look for children to fill those vacant spots. By using the new enrollment tool it allowed me to build a list and now all I have to do is reach out to those parents to see if they are still interested in childcare from our facility and 85% still are. Most of them will wait or have children in a temporary facility until you open your doors.

How you keep your office space will also determine how your day will go! You want to walk into your office or office space and not feel overwhelmed just by stepping in there already. Your office space should be like your home your safe serene place. You should love to be in your workspace and get your daily tasks done. This is impossible if your space is cluttered and unorganized, you are not focused or you cannot perform at your best self. Most likely you won't get as much work done either.

Being organized isn't a skill and it has to be practiced, we all don't have the gift of organization. It took me sometime to grasp the concept of getting organized and creating strategies to keep my business organized. It is a difference between setting up your daily task or to do list and keeping organized, then there is time management. Yes, it is possible to only have mastered 2 out of the 3 or even just one area! You must stay focused and create boundaries and strategies to accomplish all 3. When you figure it out you will realize it's not rocket science. After finding out what is best for you and works just stick to it.

Set aside binders for your paperwork. Each area should have its own topic. Each staff including yourself should have a binder with all the necessary paperwork, clearances, trainings etc. This makes it easier for inspectors when they come into your facility to just hand them your binders and they can look through them faster then just giving them a folder with papers all over the place. The less questions they have to ask the less time they will be in your facility. We all want them in and out not a minute pass what they need to be there for.

Having your items organized also helps in being prepared for inspection rather they are scheduled or pop ups. If you stay ready it's not as difficult to get ready. You should have staff meetings monthly covering specific topics. At least one to two times a year one of those meetings should be going over staff files. Get your staff involved in this process don't do it all yourself, this also helps your staff appreciate and know what all goes into their position and the importance of keeping up with State and municipal requirements.

You will see a big difference in the way your business runs once you put everything into perspective. Have dates in place for checking children's files as well. I typically do my child files every April and October no matter when the child enrolled. This helps me keep up with what child needs new health forms and periodic reviews of their files. Personalize your routine toward your needs and staff needs.

What tasks do you need to organize in your business?

_____

_____

_____

_____

_____

_____

_____

_____

_____

_____

_____

_____

_____

What materials do you need to implement them?

_____

_____

_____

_____

_____

_____

_____

_____

_____

_____

The difference between

ordinary and extraordinary is the little extra.

-Jimmy Johnson

Passion

When something is your passion you don't have to search for it. Your passion is your life. You breathe it, feel it and live in it. As I said before your passion has to be practiced or you will lose it. We have to reach deep down to find out what our real passion is. We may like or enjoy doing a number of activities however what areas in your life you just couldn't live without? If it was taken from you, you would be miserable.

Your passion should make you happy. If you have to, reconnect with your dreams. Each day you should be creating in your passion. In other words' fueling your passion. If you have identified your passion, are you giving it attention every day? You have to grow in your passion. Getting out of your comfort zone will help you expand in your passion and as a human being. Challenge yourself and do some soul searching to help you reach your full understanding of your passion. You should also be evolving so your passion doesn't get boring to you.

Get quiet sometimes and process internally how your passion should be reflected in your life. Your passion is what you tap into when you feel like you have no reason, when you feel depressed, when your not focused. If you are not using your passion you feel worthless. Study your passion and make your life match what your passion is in your mind. Never give up on your passion even if your blueprint doesn't match just revamp it.

You have the power to do anything you desire in your life. Think about what you can do to bring your passion out. It can be writing it out, saying affirmations and mantras etc. Set goals to make your environment conducive to your growth. You should always find ways to feed your mind and talent. The best thing is we get to turn our passion into a business! What's better than getting paid for doing what you love! Your passion is discovered and you have to gain mastery within it. We don't always know what our passion is right away. You should get excited about your passion! I know when I speak about anything that I am passionate about I turn into a big baby! No, I really do! I get emotional about the things I care about. Your money should be invested into your passion. Creating opportunities to grow in yourself and business. Does your passion make your heart race" Do some reflection...Ask yourself what your passion is? Some know right away however for some it takes half their life to figure it out. Life is way too short to hate what you do during the day or majority of the time.

There is a way to find your passion. Many of us know what our passion is but ironically many individuals do not. The more you connect to your passion the more joy you bring to your life. That's a proven fact. You need to have a reason for being. What are you actually good at? Think about it. What can you contribute to the world and what can you get paid for? So where do you start right! Was there ever a time you were in your element and how you felt so incredible! Just being conscious and aware of this feeling will help you figure out your purpose and passion. Here's what you can do make a chart and divide the paper in to 4 sections. The first box write out all the things you love to do and are good at these are your passions. The second write out what you don't love but are still good at, these things pay the bills! The third box write what you love but are not good at this is your potential. Something that if you worked on and had guidance in you would excel in. And lastly what you don/t love and what you're not good at these are your daily tasks. We tend to focus on what we don't love and are not good at and what we don't love but are good at. However, its ok but we need to increase our time to work on what we deserve and the lifestyles we want to create. We never put in the time to identify. We have to make time even if it's on the weekend. The goal is to make your passion your paycheck. That also requires daily investment and learning.

Yes, we may know it but we need to go further in our mastering. Remember you're never too old to learn or too rich to be taught. The world is always revolving so don't ever get stuck keep up with what's going on in the world.

Write out what you love and are good at.

_____

_____

_____

_____

_____

_____

Write out what you don't love but are good at.

_____

_____

_____

_____

_____

Write out what you love but are not good at.

_____

Write out what you don/t love and are not good at.

_____

_____

_____

_____

_____

_____

_____

Quality vs. Quantity

Let's take pens for instance. We buy pens and we buy lots of them. We have them laying around our office, our homes and even our vehicles. We don't care if we lose one because we have plenty more where they came from. So, if one gets broken or misplaced it/s no big deal because we have plenty right! However, you have pens that are very high tech, they write very smoothly, they have refillable ink cartridges and you use that same pen for everything. Out of those two pens I can guarantee you would rather the second one.

There are three rules to high quality. It needs to be unique, there is nothing else out there like it and make an impact. And it also has to be of good quality. We know how to make ideas and bring them out to the world but It must do something meaningful. And lastly it enhances people's life.

Think of childcare as those pens. There are so many childcare facilities set up just about on every block. They all do the basics and get the job done. Each program has the usual…offer meals, same hours of operation, "high quality care", a curriculum, teachers etc. Since there are so many types of pens out there what would make someone spend the extra money on your pen? What does this particular pen do differently and why would I not pick a pen like bic which has so many different pens out there and is even known.

So in other words yes there are plenty of childcare facilities out here however what is your green apple? My Ex(sell)ing your Mind, Business and Vision Mastermind attendees you know what I'm speaking of! Sometimes It not about how many of something you have but about making what you have of quality. So many people are hooked on trying to open number 2,3,4 and Number 1 isn't even in good standards or able to strive at Its best potential. Because they think by having multiple facilities means their winning and that's not the truth at all. I'd rather have 1 or 2 facilities that I know are manageable and I can stretch my time between the two of them.

I know my limit and I want to be present and active in my facilities so two is my limit. You some want to spread yourself too thin. Unless you're going to hire a director to over see your facility. If you're like me I am hands on in my businesses and I want to keep all of my coins OKAY!

It's easy to get caught up in the hype when you see so many facilities popping up and providers having multiple facilities. Please believe many of them do not succeed because they haven't done the research on or realized the work that goes into operating multiple facilities. I always feel like when I have my center location where I want it to be and everything is running smoothly, I have to attend to my family daycare. Then I'm at my family daycare and my center is slacking off. That is the reason why I implemented

Task Management Binders into my business practice. There is no reason why my facilities both cannot run smoothly without me being present. It also has a lot to do with your team. You have to have a tight supportive team, but we will speak on that in the Staff chapter.

What can you do in your facility to make it stand out from the rest of other childcare businesses?

_____

_____

_____

_____

_____

_____

_____

_____

_____

If you don't PAY

you won't PAYattention

-Coach STORMY WELLINGTON

Reinvest in Yourself

What kind of investment have you made in you? If you plan on being the best of the best you have to take away somethings just as much as you have to put into yourself. Are you being affective in your works? Are you using your time sufficiently? You can have more than you are if you work on yourself........personal development! The greatest investment you can ever make is in yourself. You are your greatest asset and will carry yourself a long way, Most of the things we need to know we already know, it lies inside of us and just needs to be ignited.

You should be reading as we talked about before at least 6 books a year. The more knowledge you learn the more you can apply to your life and your work. Invest in events. Attend different event that are not only in childcare but also in areas that you enjoy. Remember your life should be well rounded you need to nurture all the areas in your life that make up who you are. I attend workshops, trainings, seminars, learning group and all that are geared toward childcare and staying in the loop and involving myself in the Early Childhood community. However, there are many other things I am interested in. I enjoy going to empowerment seminars and working on expanding my thought process and how people operate. I engage in at least 3 personal seminars a year to keep myself focused and inspired. That's the only way I can continue to inspire you guys. As the saying goes you can't pour from an empty cup! Every time I attend one of these events I always come back fired up! I am ready to go and I have so many ideas that I am always excited about sharing and presenting to all my supporters.

You should not be thinking with your fixed mindset telling yourself " I don't have the money for that class or book". You should be thinking with a growth mindset and say to yourself , "How can I attend this class, I have to find a way to invest into this class". A growth mindset will figure it out later and just go for it and take that leap of faith. You should be saying instead I don't have the money NOT to go to that event or I don't have the time NOT to read that book, That's what people that want to grow do. They change how they think and speak. They make investments not pay for things. Being an entrepreneur is all about taking a leap of faith. Having faith is believing in something you cannot see and that is exactly what starting a business is like.

I also attend seminars that are held out of town. Those are my favorite ones to attend! Believe it or not I go by myself to these events because I don't have time waiting on people procrastinating because then you will miss out. How many times have you wanted to attend an event and you asked your friend to go with you and they say sure but now your waiting on them to come up with their part of the money or book their flight or accommodations. They keep giving you the run around and before you know it it's the week of the event and you haven't purchased a ticket or your accommodations, now you're looking at pictures and videos from the event on social media wishing you were there. I made a vow to myself that I would never be that person again and I realized that everyone will not have the ambition that I have or want to succeed as bad as I do.

I have never had a bad experience going to seminars by myself. I always meet other people that are so nice and to your surprise you will find that you are not the only one that attended alone. I have meet some of my best relationships to date in other cities (Hey Tanisha Hey Natalie)!! Plus I want to have friends that we have to make trips to visit each other don't you?! My relationship levels change as I go through the journeys that I face in life. I have better discernment these days and know how to place people in my life if at all.

Another way to invest in yourself is by receiving coaching. Coaching will dramatically improve your results and help you with or even eliminate those hiccups you may come into contact with. You will get results quicker with a Co . When you want to increase the time of learning and get your competency level up you get a coach. I love this part of what I do in my company. I enjoy seeing people want something and having the privileged to help people reach their goals or potential heights in their business. If you don't plan on leveling yourself up then there is no need for you to obtain a coach.

So there are things you can do to invest back into yourself. Change your way of speaking, invest in books to read, attend seminars and get a coach or mentor. Investing in yourself makes you happier and more skilled, We focus on the things we are good at and most likely that means that other areas are suffering in your life. Getting things never make you happy but progress gets you going, How much is your life worth and are you willing to invest to get to the life that you dream of? It's really simple if you want your life to change you have to change and if you want a different life you have to be different.

Name some ways you will reinvest

into yourself.

Two Books I will read this year.......

_____

_____

_____

_____

_____

_____

2 seminars/workshops I will attend this year

_____

_____

_____

_____

_____

_____

CONTACT

INEEZE "CHILDCARE BOSS" GAINEY

FOR A CONSULTATION OR COACHING

AT INFO@IAGCONSULT.COM

NO ONE IS GOOD AT

EVERYTHING, BUT EVERYONE

IS GOOD AT SOMETHING.

-UNKNOWN

Staff

In an ideal world we would all have the perfect staff.

Everyone would be on bored and know exactly what our

visions are and how important it is to make sure they stay

on task and utilized the management skills we worked so

hard on creating and implementing. We usually have a

team made up of different personalities and work traits.

What we are looking for we will never find in just one

person. Just like you lack in areas so will your staff

therefore you will need to hire team members like putting

together a puzzle. You may have someone with strong

teaching skills or another that is great in leadership or

multi-tasking, an organizer or a team player. This is where

your leadership skills kick in and you have to use your

skills to place those people where they will strive the most.

When hiring staff you want to look for special elements in

people, Skill, company and job. Get a good job description

on each type of position you are looking for. A resume should cover their skill, knowledge and experience for the job. Of course, verifying these skills is a must. Company fit deals with if a person will fit with the team and the company. Job fit is tricky because you can only see the surface of the person, you can't really see how a potential employee works until they are on the job. Thats why its important to ask specific questions and having an assessment tool and also calling them back for a mock interview, This way you can see how they work with the children and the other staff. If they are stand offish or they jump right in.

Hire the most qualified candidates for the position and make sure they are will to elevate. Assure they are coachable and can take direction as well as give direction. Hardworking employees offer the best chance for success. I need people on my team that will think of my business as their own. We are all in this together and if we fail as a team the business fails too. I expect if they see something out of place to jump right in and be of an assistance, not to wait for me to address it first.

However, I have realized that people don't want to work! So, you must be creative in pulling people in to your business and keeping them. We have a lot of turnover in the childcare industry. So, when you find those people you want to keep them. You should have training in place for your staff. Use different types of training, make them convenient but also informative and change up the style of training. Utilize the internet but also get out and attend trainings and also have trainings come to your staff. And explain to them that they will be required to do a certain amount of training hours. Feed them and play games to loosen up the atmosphere. If your staff is not adequately trained they will not understand or enjoy the job. Happy staff equal higher profits.

You have to attract the type of people you want on your team just like you attract the things you want into your life it's no difference! Think about the type of person you want to work for you and write down their qualities and strengths and ambition. Get out and interact with other providers in your community and organizations. You won't get far by staying secluded. I'm glad to say that one of the great parts about social media is the connections that can be made between providers not just in your city but all over the world. Providers are beginning to get out of the mindset of another provider being their competition and instead a support system. Children come and go but there are plenty of children for all of us to care for. And children are not going out of style!

Just as you have an ongoing list of children that you created by continuously doing tours wether you are full or not. You should do the sane for staff so that when a staff person leaves or quits your not in a crisis and are panicking to fill that position.

Make your staff feel appreciated. No one wants to be anywhere and feel that they are valued or appreciated for their hard word. Reward them for any good jobs they are doing. Just a simple horn toot goes along way. A simple thank you or I appreciate you for that can make someone's day! Have a staff appreciation day and congratulate a special staff member. Give them a certificate or something tangible that they can look back at.

Get personal with your staff. See what it is that they love to do and show them that you are interested in their likes and needs too. When you show them that it's not just all about you and making sure that you get what you want, they will appreciate you even more and respect you on another level. Personalize gifts you give to them. Let the staff pick places to have meetings and engagements at. Involve them and make them feel like they really matter.

Here is my vision for the staff I want to attract to my

childcare business:

_____

_____

_____

_____

_____

_____

_____

_____

_____

_____

_____

_____

SCARED MONEY DON'T MAKE NO MONEY!

-MEEK MILL

Tax Preparation

The time of the year we all dread. Well I know I do! I have been doing my taxes for 13 years now in my business and it still doesn't seem to get easier. Taxes can be very scary and confusing. I always felt like they would never tell me that I over paid and they would keep my money! However, I was doing my taxes all wrong for many years. Trying to beat the system and being brainwashed to always make them think you make less than what you really were so you could catch a break. I didn't realize that was really hurting my business in the long run.

Let me be transparent for a moment I was not reporting cash payments or payments from parents that never asked for the summary form at the end of the year. However, I have learned over the years the do's and don'ts of Tax preparation. I use to put all my receipts in a bin, then when I was ready to do my taxes I had to single handedly calculate my expenses by hand. I would make the categories of my expenses and sit with my calculator and a pen and paper. One by one I would add these receipts up. Some of you witnessed this on my Instagram LIVE!

Preseason tax prep is essential and will relieve plenty of stress. You should tally up everyone of your expenses for your business. You should begin this starting October or even better yet as you make purchases keep track of your records or at least monthly. You can use a software system or app to help with this I personally like WAVES its very easy. You simply download to your phone and use as you go after making a transaction in a store and the APP places it in the correct category and adds up your total throughout the year.

You can also use quick books or use a book keeping company to keep you on track. You would simply provide all your expenses and receipts to them and they will do all of the categorizing and strategizing for you. You should have a great record keeping system set up for your business.

Here is a list of expenses that you can create categories for. Supplies, entertainment, payroll, gas, auto, insurance, mortgage, travel expenses, meal, interest fees, home expenses, electricity, utilities, legal and professional expenses, advertising etc. The list can go on and one. These are everyday expenses in your business. As long as you can turn them into legit business deducted expenses. Having taxable income is another and also knowing the difference between credits and deductions. With the right tax professional they can maximize and identify all the credits you qualify for.

If your childcare facility is in your home you get to deduct your insurance, property tax, rent, utilities and more. Also if you have a car you can write off your mileage and gas used during your business hours. You can even get deductibles for the maintenance, tires and vehicle expenses.

Deducting meals and entertainment you can utilize from business meetings or business benefit. Every time you treat your staff to lunch or purchase food for meeting and events you have for your staff. Operational expenses can be gifts you give to your employees and their uniforms and even image maintenance, Cell phone expenses too.

Here's another one hiring your children! Yes hire your kids and make them work in your business and get a tax deduction. Children between the ages of 7-17 receive up to a $6,100 per child tax free deductible! Children are not subject to payroll taxes. However, there are rules of course! You must have a W-9 on file for the child, provide a 1099 for the income paid and create a contract for services performed by the child!

Make sure you are conducting your business as a legal business. Get a DBA or Fictitious name. Get an EIN for your business from the IRS and open a business account.

DO NOT COMMINGLE! Get separate bank account for your business.

Create those systems implement them. Have a system for storing your receipts. Plan a day once a month where you can go through your receipts and sort and file them. Dedicate that day strictly for this purpose. Make sure to look through your emails, take your milage intake and monthly utilities. Again categorize them standard, non-standard and checks. I love Minute Menu pro its specifically for childcare providers and has many resources that will keep you on track with your expenses.

Decide if you are going to be Sole proprietor, LLC or S Corp. Sole Proprietor is okay However best practice would be to file as a LLC or S Corp. Here is a simple break down of the difference between the two. Both are actually LLC's. A LLC is taxed as a sole proprietor and a S Corp is taxed as so. Both provide legal protection and have operational advantages and the profits and losses will flow through to the business owner. Your Net profit is what's left from your business expenses and deductions off the gross income. With an LLC your entire net profit will be subject to self employment tax which is about 15.3 percent then you'll be subject to pay State and Federal Income Tax. When you incorporate to a S Corp you take two forms of income. The first is that you pay yourself a salary and the second part is a distribution or dividend. The salary is subject to the Self Employment tax of 15.3 percent while the distribution is not. So now your saving but be careful not to falsely shift things over to your salary side. Your salary has to be reasonable. Now if you are already an LLC no worries you can file for an S –Election. But do it before your taxes are due. Speak to your CPA to explain more in debt.

What system will you use or are you using to keep track of your receipts?

_____

_____

_____

_____

_____

_____

_____

_____

_____

What are your Expenses?

Gas_____

_____

Food_____

_____

Supplies_____

_____

Equipment_____

_____

Car

Expenses_____

_____

Utilities_____

_____

Mortgage_____

_____

Entertainment_____

_____

Other_____

_____

_____

THE HUMAN MIND IS OUR

FUNDAMENTAL RESOURCE.

-UNKNOWN

Utilizing the Resources Around You

Being in business is about accessing resources as much as you can. You want to keep those resources accessible to you. One way is to take control over something you can control which is your credit. The more credit you have the more leverage and power you have. Take advantage of using someone else's money and not your own. Another resource is tools and software. Think about what your needs are in your business. Having tools and software for your business can help you out drastically. Find out what is difficult for you in your business and find a tool or software app for it there are millions that are available and most of them are free.

Social media is an amazing resource if it is used correctly. It can help to grow your business, create relationships and give you exposure for your new business. Whichever platform works best for you utilize it. I prefer Instagram but my account is also connected to facebook which I love because I hate having to post on each page separately.

Yes you can benefit from Instagram in your childcare business. Your account should be set up as a business account. Having a business account gives you more access to do things that regular accounts can't do. You can track how many views your page receives if people are clicking on your website link and so much more. Use your explore page to find and follow like people and accounts. When you like posts of things you like and are interested in Instagram will generate your explore page of more of those interests for you.

Social Media will also expand your business quickly to potential clients that are outside of your city or town even state. I have met many people through social media and it has been amazing! I've created relationships that probably would not have transpired if it were not for the social media platform. Social Media has given me that boost that I needed to get my consulting business up and running the way I envisioned it and to make my presence known.

There are many resources in the childcare field you just have to make yourself aware and be connected. Depending on the state that you are in their should be a quality program that either you are mandated to be involved in or an optional source. Many facilities don't want to be involved with these resources because they don't want them in their programs and browsing around. I totally understand however do your research on these programs and see what the major purpose is and how can it be of a benefit to you. If you need technical support or support within your program and staff that can help extremely.

I take advantage of many programs and am proud to be a part of them. The programs that my facilities partake in I wouldn't mind recommending so I know I like them a lot. They contribute to my vision and help me to keep my staff on task and it's always good for your staff to hear the same things that you have been trying to tell them come from someone else! Some of them also offer funding with grants that you can use for the children and your staff which is always exciting. They even offer funding for your staff to further their education which I think is so amazing. I wish I worked for a program that paid for my degrees I wouldn't be in debt with student loans now! Thank God I am almost done!

There are also resources to help you assess your business and see if you are using best practice within your business. It scores you just as if you were doing an assessment on a child and it reveals your best and not so great areas of your business. Making sure that you have the correct paperwork and your implementing these actions into your business. My favorite business assessment tool is the BAS Tool. It guides you through every aspect of your business from policies, communicating with your parents and staff benefits for your staff and record keeping. I found this tool very helpful because it had items listed that I had never thought of using in my business but it made sense.

You need to stay connected with a group or club of some kind. Sign up for a membership with your local childcare organizations and community groups. Plenty of funding gets funneled through these organizations and because you are linked to them that puts you in the pathway to receive funds too. I have so many opportunities that come across my desk from start up funding, free or low cost equipment, other providers selling their business or items just by being connected to the childcare world in my city.

It is also great to be in the know when major announcements come down the pipeline you are one of the first to find out. This gives you lead way to get a head start on implementing them into your facility and for staff.

So do you still want to stay in that bubble of yours in your business when you can get out and connect and network and benefit from these many programs.

What organizations or groups can you join in your State or region?

_____

_____

_____

_____

_____

_____

_____

_____

What social media platforms are you using and how can you utilize them to grow exposure for your business and more clients?

_____

_____

_____

_____

_____

_____

_____

_____

LIFE FAILURES ARE WHAT BUILDS CHARACTER.

ENDURE YOUR FAILURES WITH GRACE IT'S NOT

ABOUT THE PAIN IT'S MORE ABOUT THE LESSON.

THE LESSON IS THE BLESSING. WHAT YOU LEARN

WILL TEACH YOU WHAT TO DO IN LIFE OR WHAT NOT

TO DO IN LIFE.

-BRADLEY "TUFFY" TORRENCE

Values of being a Boss

What does being a boss mean to you? Is it just about being in control or dictating to people what they can and cannot do? Do you drive your staff or are you coaching them. Do you blame your employees for breakdowns or do you just jump in and fix the break down. Are you commanding or asking your staff to complete tasks? Are you using people for personal gain or are you developing people? Are you inspiring fear into your staff or generating enthusiasm? What about taking credit from your staff and not giving them credit for their work ethic and ideas. How do you speak is "I" only on your vocabulary or do you speak more of "We". Me personally I call myself a Boss but I look at myself as more of a leader.

What are the major practices of leadership that we must enact on an everyday bases to have the amount of influence and impact we desire in our work lives or any role in which we are leading other people. Great leaders envision a different future than what is here. They have a clear view of what the world can be like tomorrow than it is today. Leaders have a shattered purpose that they believe themselves and others will be inspired by this vision. It's a practice of envisioning what should tomorrow be like and look like for my team. Enlist other people to share their perspective, voices, dreams and desire. If people are involved in creating a vision they will support it. Great leaders are constantly asking what do others need and want and what would they like to see. Great leaders are always embodying their message. What they are saying and how they behave. Leaders also empower people. This is by far my favorite thing to do! To just connect and listen to a person and give them the tools, technology, training and coaching they need to allow them to succeed really warms my heart. That's what empowering is about. You have many bosses that come in and have a big vision to get everyone involved but don't equip their team to kick ass. This happens often. You have to be consistent with your training and coaching of your staff. We also need to evaluate the key people that are with us and evaluate their needs and skills and contributions and ethics. Are we being ethical in our evaluation. That's one of the hardest things to do. And of course we have to encourage our team its vital. We must be the cheerleader, inspirer and champion. Always be the person to uplift and light people up and get them excited about things. You need to have it in your heart and in your soul to want to encourage people. Even when it's hard. When you're working towards a goal, the more conflict, the doubt, the more the challenge leaders have to deal with them by being that voice. When it gets dark your solid you're always going to turn a negative into a positive and they know they can go to you. We must respect each other. When you get people to collaborate with you it's not just you anymore it's a team and they now are helping with your vision and they are now standing for something and encouraging so it's not just on your shoulders.

What are you doing to be more of a leader than a boss?

_____

_____

_____

_____

_____

_____

_____

_____

How are you encouraging your staff?

_____

How are you making an impact in other peoples

lives?

_____

_____

_____

_____

_____

_____

_____

I WILL NEVER STOP

-WALLO267

WHY (Your Big Why)

First thing that comes to mind is money for many, and if that was you you need to dig a little deeper. Your WHY should keep you up at night and eager to begin your day in the morning. You should want to take desperate measures for your WHY! My WHY is my son and to never be broke another day in my life.

My son is my only child. I try to be an example for him to show him that hard work does pay off like my mother showed me. I want him to see and know that you have to fight your way to the top in this world and make yourself known.

This is a cold cold world and he will find out in due time. However my place is to make sure that reality will be of no concern to him. My goal is to have him set up for life and equipped with wealth and knowledge way ahead of his time. I worry so much about him and how he will navigate through his life. I know I have to step back and allow him to learn and that's the hardest part. I remember struggling all through my life. Being a young child living in a shelter. Wearing hand me downs and donated clothes and shoes. Not having my own room ever until I purchased my first home as an adult.

I remember going to bed hungry and couldn't wait to goto school the next day just to have a meal. From working paycheck to paycheck and barely being able to put gas in my car to get to work.

Having to decide what bills should I pay and what bills will just have to wait. I was always an earner though and willing to work. I begged my mother at 14 to take me to get my working papers. I hustled whatever I could get my hands on everything was for sell.

I promised myself I would never be in that situation again. College was my breakout. I never looked back after that. I was smart about some decision but I also had lessons presented to me and I Am grateful for every last one.Im not one to ask a person for anything, I would rather go without it figure It out. No one ever knows if I'm struggling because I make It look so damn good. I've had my trying times and we all do but it's all in how you deal with situations. God continued to bless me through my good and bad times and those lessons made me stronger and built a strong back. Selling dinners to make ends meet, posting up a water ice and candy stand. Working with my father in north Philly at his crab shack and fruit and vegetable truck, driving around from neighborhood to neighborhood. I wasn't ashamed when It came to making my money. I did what was necessary. I didn't want to be a statistic or on welfare. I had to break the cycle.

What is your Big WHY?

_____

_____

_____

_____

_____

_____

Experience is the teacher of all things

-Julius Caesar

XX11

I am truly blessed to be able to follow my dreams and do what I have always set out to do and more! 22 is the number of years that I have been in the Early Childhood field. I started at a young age watching over my siblings. Having a mother that went out to work to provide for her children in a single family household. My mother worked 24 hour shifts 2 to 3 times out of the week. Leaving us to grow up and learn how to be independent quickly. I love my mother dearly and I know she did the best she could for us. She had no education having to drop out of school at a very young age herself to take care of her siblings as a young girl in St. Lucia. My mother had the opportunity to go back and volunteer at the same shelter we once lived in and they offered her a job. This meant she could get on her own feet and provide for her family but also that we wouldn't see our mother for a day or two. I have always been the nurturer in my family. My older sister left the house when I was about 10 or 11 years old. I became the older sister looking after my siblings while my mother went to work. That was my foundation.

Fast forward I always took a liking to children and nurturing them. I learned that role of being a nurturer at a very young age. I just knew in my heart that my calling was to do a service to children and give them opportunities that were never presented or exposed to me. I actually began my college journey as a Pre Medicine Major but quickly realized that wasn't the field for me! I switched my major to Early Childhood Education and I felt really comfortable and in my element. I really enjoyed learning how to teach children and using my creativity. I excelled in college and was very competitive. I was a different person when it came to getting into the mind of a child. Seeing their faces light up when you tap into something that interests them and you give them your undivided attention. My senior year at Lincoln University I had to complete my practicum. I decided to stay home that last semester because I was expecting my son so I wanted to be close to home. I completed my practicum at a bilingual school in North Philadelphia. That was the best feeling I had ever had. I loved working with those children and most of them could barely speak english but that made the challenge even more superb. I enjoyed the class that I had and my leading teacher was amazing Ms. Easley I think her name was I asked her so many questions about being a teacher and the school and her colleagues she probably thought I was crazy! I remember it was assessment time and Ms. Easley allowed me to conduct the assessments. I recall her giving me instruction on how to conduct the assessments and telling me that I could not help the children in anyway even if I knew that they knew the answer. There were other times we were teaching lessons and I would go to her with suggestions of activities to possibly do with the children and she quickly stopped me and said they won't allow that. I immediately thought to myself who is THEY? She explained how this particular school district is very adamant about teaching the kids the way the lesson plans are laid out with no room to recreate . This broke my heart because I knew that all these children do not learn the same and on top of that their second language is english so they already have a setback. From that moment I realized that I wouldn't be able to work for the school district and decided to open up my own facility. I graduated with my Bachelors of Science in Elementary Education and a Minor in Early childhood Education. I worked for a Robotics program during the summer, then after having my son I began to work for a Behavioral Health facility for children. I was placed in an Autism Spectrum classroom in the school district which I worked for about 3 years. Then I decided it was time to plan to start my dream of opening-up my own daycare. I stumbled and didn't know what direction to go in. I did plenty of research and even tried to reach out to a few people to give me some guidance. That was always a dead end. For some reason providers weren't willing to talk to me about the childcare business or would just give me false information and have me running all around the city to the wrong facilities. Until I came across a young lady that to this day we are still connected I call her my sister in fact. I was looking for childcare for my son and she was placed in my path by God. Not only did she have one spot left she was willing to give me the ropes on the childcare business just enough to get me on track and moving in a direction that would change my life forever.

I started off with my family childcare facility and grew that for 10 years. I learned so much from the many families I provided a service to as well as business practices. I didn't know the first thing about running a business other than what was taught to me in college but that really doesn't help! YOU HAVE TO LEARN WHILE YOU OPERATE! Many people think they have to know or have everything in place to start their business, which is not true. That type of thinking will actually destroy your business before you even begin. You can learn in your business then as you grow you then tweak and change or implement in to the business. I was very grateful that I was privileged to have the opportunity and means to open up as a family daycare. I believe this gave me the opportunity to grow and perfect my business and make mistakes on a smaller scale to prepare for my center. I have provided care for so many children I have lost count but I know its somewhere around the 60's and I am very appreciative of that.

I eventually knew it was time to expand I had a wait list of about 25 kids so the need was definitely there. I also began to feel like I knew I had more to offer than what I was giving in my home and wanted more children to experience that. I opened the doors of my center in 2015. It is a struggle at times but I wouldn't give it up for the world! I found myself communicating with other providers more and answering questions and helping them out. An opportunity arose where I became a Mentor for the Keystone Stars Program. I was very familiar with

Keystone Stars and my facility is a Star 4A (Accredited) which is the highest level. I met some great ladies and helped them with their goals then suddenly like many good things it came to an end because funding was cut. I realized I really enjoyed being behind the scenes and meeting new providers and helping them create and accomplish goals in their facilities! Thats when I decided to take a leap of faith and do what God had been calling on me to do! I have been helping woman alike now for 3 years, 2 years within my own company and assisting over 158 childcare providers and opening start to finish 13 childcare facilities! I truly love what I do and I don't feel like I'm working! I enjoy giving back and making an impact on peoples lives especially woman. I'm such a feminist! I plan on adding

another 10-20 years to my already 22!

What have you learned in the years that you have

devoted your time to Early Childhood and

development?

_____

_____

_____

_____

_____

_____

_____

_____

Edit your life frequently and ruthlessly.

It's your Masterpiece after all.

-Unknown

Year End Evaluation

It never fails every time It gets close to the end of the year we begin to look at our lives and begin to evaluate what we have done or not done that year. We create "New Year Resolutions", think about the relationships and friends in our lives that we need to tarnish and how we are not going to let people treat us a certain way and dictate our lives blah blah blah.

So why don't you do that for your business? This is a great time to evaluate your business as well. Think about how your business ran for the past year, what did you incorporate or change and may w eliminated. Did It work or It was a flop? Think about your staff have they been a good fit or is It time to make some changes?

Start with your paperwork and review the systems you have been using. What about marketing, has whatever you have in place been beneficial or is It time to use another approach? What about your curriculum? Are the children learning and growing from it? Any policies need to be revised or implemented? Now evaluate yourself as a leader. Have you held up your part of the bargain? Are you keeping your staff encouraged and accountable. What can you change or increase about your leadership skills? And don't be afraid to have your staff evaluate you just as you evaluate them or even each other this can be done anonymously!

If there is a Book you wanna read, But it hasn't been written yet; then write it.

-Toni Morrison

ZEAL

I know God has a bigger calling on my life and I accept it. There is so much that I want to accomplish in this childcare mainstream that I haven't even touched yet. I am willing to get out here and grind and hustle to accomplish what God has put me on earth to complete. I believe that I am walking in the write steps and path. I get such a comforting feeling when I help another individual get closer to their goal or even establish something they thought was not possible. When you have a calling on you you don't sleep your always up creating and thinking how to out do yourself. Im constantly thinking of new material to bring to my clients and followers. I know that someone is looking for me to post a message or uplift them by simply responding to a Dm and yes I answer all of them! When God takes you through things he doesn't take you through it to keep it a secret. I believe I am here to help people find that light within themselves to believe in what their purpose is. I can honestly say I know my Path of Meaning! I am a contributor. I feel like the work I am doing is more than myself. It is very invigorating when you know what your life is about.when you achieve a higher purpose. Its not about making money to me because I have put out mote than I have received , I have also lost out on more money than I have received. I know my vision will get through to many and I plan on touching as many people as I can. I have interacted and set goals that I would never have imagined me doing in a hundred years! This book is one of them. People always say the sky is the limit but I beg to differ I believe your mind is your limit. Have that one thing or multiple things you want to pursue that is what zeal is and go after it. Write them down and tackle them one by one. Expect your mind and vision to change each time you level up. I don't entertain nor care to involve myself into many situations, I chose to do things that stimulate my mind. I expect more for myself therefore I expect more for you too. Until you get that feeling and know it, My job isn't done!

Wha are you pursuing in your life? What is your Zeal and

How do you plan on achieving it?

_____

_____

_____

_____

_____

_____

_____

_____

_____

_____

Thank you for supporting my Dream by purchasing my first book! You will be heading and seeing more of me! My purpose just got BIGGER!

-Childcare Boss